Music School Mastery

Building Your Academy for Budding Musicians

Table of Contents

Chapter 1. Introduction

Welcome aboard a harmonious journey that will strike a chord with your entrepreneurial spirit and passion for music. Our exclusive Special Report, 'Music School Mastery: Building Your Academy for Budding Musicians', hums the melody of mastery, guiding you step-by-step on how to create that haven where gifted novices blossom into accomplished musicians. Not a deeply technical discourse, but rather, a vivid symphony of proven strategies, hands-on advice, and heartwarming anecdotes, this report is your backstage pass to launching and nurturing your very own music academy. By the time these pages cease to turn, you'll be ready to strike the right note with your venture. So, make your passion your crescendo and let this enlightening report inspire your encore!

Chapter 2. Setting the Stage: Blueprint of a Successful Music Academy

First things first, you cannot build a successful music academy without a solid blueprint. The architecture of your business plays a crucial role in determining its future success. So, without further ado, let's delve into the anatomy of an inspiring and flourishing music school.

2.1. The Concept: Identifying Your Unique Selling Proposition

Every effective plan begins by defining the 'why.' What sets your music school apart from the rest? Is it your innovative approach to teaching, or perhaps your specialized program focusing on specific genres?

Clearly identifying your Unique Selling Proposition (USP) will give you an edge in an increasingly crowded market. Conduct market research to understand the demand and uncover gaps that your academy could fill. Flexibility, niche classes, and exceptional instructors might all be part of your USP. Once defined, your USP will form the cornerstone of your music academy's identity and marketing strategy.

2.2. The Curriculum: Polishing Your Pedagogical Approach

The backbone of any music school is its curriculum. Traditional music schools may adhere strictly to recognized syllabi, such as

ABRSM or Trinity, while others may choose to innovate and develop their specific programs.

Consider your target demographic and their needs. Young children may enjoy a mix of theory and practical learning, with a strong emphasis on play and exploration. Meanwhile, adult learners might prefer a combination of one-on-one tuition and group workshops to delve into specific techniques or genres.

Your curriculum should sync with your USP. For instance, if your USP revolves around teaching music production, your curriculum could include lessons on software such as Ableton and Pro Tools, mixing, mastering, and even the business aspects of music production.

Remember that your curriculum needs to evolve over time. Consistently reviewing and refining your approach keeps you relevant and ensures that your teaching methods are effective.

2.3. Infrastructure and Equipment: Investing in the Basics and Beyond

A harmonious learning environment sets the tone for your music academy. This means investing in adequate infrastructure and equipment to seamlessly deliver your curriculum.

Space planning, acoustic design, sound-proof practice rooms, and comfortable teaching spaces all contribute to your infrastructure. If you're pedaling towards unique classes like music production or DJing, specialized guilds are a necessity.

Selecting musical instruments depends on your curriculum. A general guide to start with includes pianos, keyboards, guitars, violins, percussion instruments, microphones, and maybe a few woodwind or brass instruments. If possible, providing a variety of instruments gives students the chance to explore and discover their preferred instrument.

Technological investments are also crucial. Setting up a basic recording studio can aid in teaching students about composition and music production. Additionally, software for administration, scheduling, and communication can ensure smooth operations and a professional student-parent interface.

2.4. Staffing: Tuning into the Right Team

Your staff is the heart that will pump life into your music academy. Thus, a meticulous procedure to recruit the right blend of administrative staff, instructors, and support staff is central.

Teachers are the limelight of your academy. Criteria for hiring should include verified qualifications, teaching experience, a dedication to students' progress, and most importantly, a shared vision for your academy.

Administrative staff must possess excellent organizational and communication skills. They are your main link to parents and students for day-to-day interactions and can significantly influence your reputation.

Support staff will ensure the efficient running of the academy. Cleaning, maintenance, and security personnel contribute to a welcoming, safe, and nurturing environment, which is paramount for learning.

2.5. Financial Planning and Pricing: Striking the Right Note

Establishing your tuition fees needs a careful balancing act. Pricing plays a significant role in your positioning. While you should gather data on what the market is charging, offering value for money is what will drive enrollment.

Keep in mind your operating costs, including but not limited to rentals, utilities, salaries, maintenance, and depreciation of equipment. Initial investments for infrastructure and equipment should also be factored into your pricing decisons.

2.6. Marketing and Networking: Creating Your Symphony

Social visibility, community building, and networking are essential. Offering workshops, open houses, and participating in local events can help you connect with potential students. Collaborating with local businesses, forming partnerships with school music programs, and offering referral benefits can also widen your reach.

Online visibility is equivalent to, if not more important than, offline visibility in the digital age. A user-friendly website, regular social media updates, newsletters, and online ads can attract prospective students.

Remember, launching a music academy is akin to conducting an orchestra. Each element outlined in the blueprint plays its part, contributing to the symphony that is your music school. The result? A thriving music academy that students enjoy, parents appreciate, and the community values. As you proceed, always attune your academy to the ever-changing rhythm and pulse of the music education landscape, and never lose sight of your mission – to create accomplished musicians.

Chapter 3. The Power Chords of Your Business Plan

Like a symphony that requires a score to guide its harmonious blend of instruments, a business plan is the guiding script for your music academy. It highlights the intricate composition of your ideas, goals, and strategies, turning them into a coherent melody of practical actions designed to accomplish your desired future.

3.1. Establishing Your Vision

To begin your business plan, you need to establish your vision. Your vision statement should be a compelling, inspiring depiction of what your music academy hopes to achieve. It should draw in your readers - potential investors, partners, or employees - and stir their excitement about the project.

Imagine your academy at its fully realized state. What are you known for? What kind of reputation do you uphold? Answering these questions will help you draft a vision that strikes a chord with anyone who engages with your music academy.

> "People don't buy what you do; they buy why you do it. What you do simply proves what you believe."
>
> — Simon Sinek

3.2. Defining Your Mission

Your mission outlines how you intend to achieve your vision. It's the melody to your lyrics, the rhythm to your rhyme - providing direction on what to do every day to obtain your goals. Your mission may include the genres you aim to teach, the teaching methods you believe in, and the unique experiences you plan to offer. A well-defined mission will harmonize with your vision, fortifying the structure of your business plan.

3.3. Crafting Your Business Objectives

Your business objectives are the quantifiable targets you aim to hit within specified timelines. They are akin to the crescendos and decrescendos in a piece of music, signifying milestones to be achieved or subdued.

Straightforward and precise, your objectives may focus on reaching a certain number of students within the first year, establishing relationships with local schools, or obtaining a specific revenue goal. Each of these objectives should be SMART: Specific, Measurable, Achievable, Relevant, and Time-bound.

3.4. Understanding Your Industry

Understanding your industry is akin to having a grasp of the musical piece you're set to perform. A comprehensive study of the music education sector, its trends, opportunities, and challenges, will form the third movement in your business plan's symphony.

Be sure to get a grip on the market size, growth rate, profitability, key success factors, among other aspects. Estimating the direction of your industry will help you plant your feet on a firm foundation that won't easily be shaken by unexpected changes.

3.5. Knowing Your Target Market

Creating a detailed portrait of your target market helps you understand what their needs are, what they value in music education, and how you can effectively reach and teach them.

Describe your typical student. They could be school children seeking supplementation for their school music programs, adults looking to pick up a new hobby, or retired individuals desiring to play the pieces they love. Divide these groups into segments, if necessary, then craft effective strategies to reach and attract each segment.

3.6. Marketing and Sales Strategy

Here, you design and document strategies to attract and keep your students, very much like a conductor who knows when to cue each instrument for a harmonious symphony.

Your marketing strategy should explain how you'll differentiate yourself from other music academies, how you'll communicate your offerings, and where you'll promote your academy to attract your target market. Meanwhile, your sales strategy should detail your sales process, including sales forecasting, lead generation, and conversion strategies.

3.7. Operational Plan

Next, harmonize all your business plan sections by orchestrating your operations guide - detailing the daily operations of your music academy. This includes your location, facilities, staffing, and management information systems.

Your operational plan is like the metronome guiding your academy in maintaining the rhythm and pace needed to achieve your goals. It keeps your operations in tempo with your vision, mission, and objectives.

3.8. Financial Projections

Finally, the climax of your business plan's symphony: the financial projections. It's the finale that illustrates how your vision, mission, business objectives, market analysis, marketing, and operational plans unite, producing a melody of projected profits.

Provide realistic financial projections, including your projected income, expenses, and profitability, for at least three years ahead. If seeking investors, include a break-even analysis, a return on investment (ROI) projection, and an exit strategy.

Although creating a business plan may seem daunting, remember that just like a musical piece, it doesn't have to be perfect from the get-go. You'll make adjustments and refinements along the way. What's important is that you have a score to guide you, to help you chart the course of your entrepreneurial concert and bring your music academy to life+.

Chapter 4. Recruitment Crescendo: Sourcing Talented Tutors

Behind every competent musician, stands a team of highly skilled and devoted music tutors. To bloom a garden of budding music maestros, you need the right team of nurturing mentors. This chapter unfolds the intricate symphony of recruiting the virtuoso musicians who will harmonize their wisdom and talent to cultivate the next breed of maestros within your academy.

4.1. The Pitch: Defining Your Requirements

Start with a crystal clear understanding of what you are looking for. Just as every music piece has its unique melodic structure and rhythm, every music academy possesses a distinctive learning environment and set of requirements. The blueprint of your ideal music tutor should be rooted in your academy's goals, teaching philosophy, and curriculum.

Identify competencies such as technical proficiency, teaching experience, and passion for mentoring – attributes vital for their potential role. Define the specialist disciplines you offer – be it classical piano, jazz saxophone, or rock guitar. Additionally, consider qualifications and accreditations you deem necessary for your faculty members to possess.

Document all these specifics in a detailed job description as it serves as an effective tuner, tuning out unqualified applicants, while resonating with the right candidates.

4.2. The Crescendo: Sourcing Music Tutors

Once your requirements are articulated, turn your focus to sourcing quality candidates.

- Music Conservatories and Universities offer a plentiful supply of qualified and passionate tutors. Developing working relationships with these institutions can launch a consistent influx of prospective tutor talent.

- Professional Networks and Music Associations can serve as reliable conduits for connecting with expert music professionals, exploring a vast stage of prospective instructors.

- Social Media and Online Platforms echo the melody of modern-day recruitment, with LinkedIn, Facebook groups, or specialized music platforms like SoundBetter or Lessonface, offering pulsating platforms teeming with talent.

- Existing Faculty can play their part in recruitment, with referrals often proving effective. Incentivizing referrals through a reward system can often turn your existing workforce into a diligent talent hunting squad.

- Music Competitions and Events serve as a harmonic hunting ground for sourcing exemplary music talent. Keep a keen eye on these events, as they present potential platforms to scout extraordinary talent.

4.3. The Audition: Evaluating Potential Tutors

Your task is far from over after sourcing potential candidates. Striking the right chord with your target audience requires testing their teaching capabilities and assessing their musical and mentoring qualities.

An intimate One-on-One Interview provides deep insight into their teaching philosophy, passion for music, and ability to mentor and inspire students. Simultaneously, a Teaching Demonstration or Audition allows them to showcase their instrument mastery and teaching style, so you can be sure they hit the right notes with your students.

Where appropriate, don't shy away from a Background and Reference Check. This lends valuable perspective on their work ethics, interpersonal bonanza, and how they've handled challenges in previous roles.

4.4. The Harmony: Long-Term Tutor Retention

Securing top-class music tutors is a challenge of its own, but retaining these tutors for the long-term is an equally compelling counter-melody. Foster a positive work environment that values their skills, solicits their opinions, and rewards their accomplishments. Develop opportunities for tutors to grow and learn, whether through professional development programs, workshops, competitive pay, or benefit schemes. Such orchestration not only retains your prized professionals but transforms them into advocates for your academy.

The role of music tutors in your academy is as crucial as that of every instrument in an orchestra. Every tutor adds to the harmony of your academy, shaping the quality of music education that your students receive, and defining your reputation as a learning institution. Equip yourself with a keen eye for talent, an understanding of your need, and a commitment to your tutors' satisfaction. This dedication will form the right recruitment crescendo to maintain a vibrant, top-class tutor roster for your music academy.

Chapter 5. Spotlight on Students: Nurturing New Musical Maestros

Music schools, at their heart, are a platform for the maturation and expansion of unique musical talents. It is the students, budding with raw talent and passion, who form the unique melody of each institution. Hence, to ensure the growth of these nascent seeds into fully bloomed maestros, the school also assumes a catalyst role, constantly striving towards creating the perfect habitat conducive to their musical evolution.

5.1. Shaping the Vision: Unleashing Student Potential

To start the caroling wheelwork of student floral, an effective starting point is to shape a vision for their potential. A vision gives students a sense of purpose, motivates them towards a common goal, and helps them view their progress through a specific lens. More than a mere educator, the school needs to become a beacon of light guiding the students through the darkness of uncertainty.

Recognizing each student's unique competencies and interests forms the building block of this vision. Use a combination of aptitude tests, one-on-one conversations, personal biographies, and observations to identify each student's strong points. Remember, the key is to listen - to their stories, passions, dreams, experiences and fears. Through this personal understanding, you tailor an appropriate vision for each student, catered specifically to uplift their unique strengths.

5.2. The Art of Motivation: Imparting Passion for Music

Igniting a passion for music in the hearts of the students is a defining factor for the success of any music school. This section explores key motivational strategies that help to spark this love for music.

Peer Influence: Harness the influence of fellow students to create a positive ripple. Organize performances, jams, or simply even pair students who have unique strengths - such as a knack for rhythms or a good ear for notes - with others who may learn from them.

Goal Setting: Set short and long-term musical goals for your students. They could range from learning a new instrument or mastering a particular piece from a beloved composer, to performing in public. Make sure the goals are challenging but achievable, to maintain motivation levels.

Positive Reinforcement: Encourage students when they achieve their set goals. Create a culture of celebrating progress, however small that may be. It is important to reinforce that mistakes are part of the deal - reminder them that every great maestro has missed a beat somewhere on the road to perfection.

5.3. Customized Curricula: Shaping Lessons around Individual Strengths

No two students are the same; generic formulas fail when we are dealing with unique talents and temperaments. A music school that aspires to nurture talent must recognize the distinctiveness of each student and tailor classes accordingly.

Assessment-Based Learning: Follow a flexible curriculum that adapts based on regular assessments of the student's skills, interests, and learning speeds.

Holistic View: Interdisciplinary approaches, when applied correctly, can significantly enhance learning outcomes. Encourage each student to see music through the lenses of history, culture, physics, and even math. These supplementary angles will grant them a deeper understanding of the mechanics and emotionally rich nature of music.

5.4. Harnessing Technology: E-Learning and Interactive methods

With technology permeating all corners of education, music schools must also tap into its potential to stay relevant in an increasingly digital world. From providing online classes and smart instrument simulators to leveraging interactive learning apps, technology can bring about a significant qualitative change.

Embrace Interactive Learning Platforms: Employ platforms that offer interactive learning experiences. Certain apps and games teach music theory, simulated instruments, and also provide resources for composing music.

Web-Based Forums: Facilitate digital spaces where students can share their compositions, seek feedback from peers and teachers, and collaborate on joint projects.

Online Masterclasses: Collaborate with renowned musicians for webinars and masterclasses. The chance to learn from the masters themselves is a strong motivational factor for students.

5.5. Nurturing School Culture: Creating an Atmosphere of Growth

A school's ethos resonates loud and clear in the ambiance it fosters. A nurturing culture encourages students to explore their musical identities without fear of judgment, embracing their unique sound even when it's not in tune with the popular beat.

Openness and Safety: Encourage openness to different genres and styles of music. Create a secure environment where students feel comfortable both in expressing themselves and in constructively critiquing others' performances.

Collaboration and Cooperation: Foster a sense of community among students. Encourage collaborative performances, book clubs, shared listening sessions, etc.

In conclusion, nurturing students to become musical maestros requires an environment that recognizes individuality, imbues technical skills with a love for music, embraces technology, and fosters a nurturing school culture. Packed with practical strategies and insightful anecdotes, this chapter will undoubtedly assist in shaping your music school into an esteemed platform for the musical charmers of tomorrow.

Chapter 6. Play the Right Notes: Curriculum Crafting Techniques

Creating the curriculum for a music academy involves more than just identifying songs for students to learn. It's about promoting a comprehensive understanding of music theory, nurturing creativity, honing technical skills, and fostering a strong emotional connection to the art of making music. Let's brush up on the process of curriculum crafting in detail, focusing on how you can orchestrate a balanced and inspiring programme for your budding musicians.

6.1. Understanding Your Students

Before drafting a curriculum, it is key to understand the demographic that your music academy caters to. The music syllabus for children will greatly differ from that designed for adults. Children are usually introduced to simpler instruments, basic techniques, and rudimentary music theory, while adult learners may require more advanced lessons, focusing on sophisticated techniques, comprehensive theory, and possibly even music production.

To understand your students, you should:

- Hold admission interviews or early sessions to gauge their skills and interests.

- Take into account their age, commitment level, and long-term objectives.

- Regularly reassess and alter learning plans in response to individual progress.

6.2. Fundamentals of Music

Regardless of instrument or style, your curriculum should begin with the basic language of music. Teaching your students the fundamentals of music theory ensures they have the foundational knowledge needed to proceed with their musical journey. Elements to include are:

- The musical alphabet and note reading

- Scales, chords, and arpeggios

- Time signatures, rhythms, and tempo

- Key signatures and circle of fifths

Developing a strong understanding of these basics can lay the groundwork for more advanced musical study.

6.3. Choosing the Right Instruments

Your curriculum should not impose any particular instrument on students but rather offer a selection of suitable options based on their abilities and preferences. While the traditional picks include piano, guitar, or violin, more unique choices could encompass saxophone, harp, or ethnic instruments like djembe, sitar, or zither.

Considerations while choosing instruments should be:

- The age and physique of the students.

- The genre of music they're inclined towards.

- Their prior experience with any instruments.

Ensure you have adequate resources and faculty to teach and support the chosen instruments.

6.4. Cultivating Technical Skills

An instrumental curriculum must focus on developing technical skills. Depending on the instrument, this might include fingering techniques, breath control, posture, articulation, and learning how to produce a good tone. It's imperative to dedicate time in the curriculum towards these aspects, as they form the building blocks of a musician's repertoire.

Items to consider while teaching technical skills:

- Repetitive exercises or etudes for practice.

- Monitoring posture and technique during lessons.

- Periodical skill assessments.

6.5. Genre Specific Approach

The variety of genres available in music is vast. From classical to rock, jazz to pop, each genre has its unique set of characteristics, theory, and technique. It's beneficial to introduce students to a variety of genres, but remember to cater to their individual preferences.

While designing a genre-specific approach:

- Introduce the predominant characteristics of each genre.

- Teach signature techniques or elements of each genre.

- Include well-known pieces from each genre for practice.

6.6. Performance Skills

Public performances are pivotal milestones in a musician's journey. They help to build confidence, put training into practice, and learn to communicate with an audience. Your curriculum should prepare students mentally and emotionally for onstage experiences.

When focusing on performance skills:

- Conduct regular in-house recitals for students.
- Create opportunities for public performances.
- Train on aspects like stage presence and overcoming stage fright.

6.7. Imbibing Creativity

The curriculum must inspire creativity and innovation. It should allow your students to experiment, improvise and compose their music. Music is a form of self-expression, and offering this exploratory freedom can be incredibly beneficial to progressive learning.

While fostering creativity:

- Encourage students to reinterpret known pieces.
- Provide lessons in basic songwriting and composition.
- Promote participation in collaborative music-making sessions.

6.8. Continuous Evaluations and Feedback

Periodic evaluations are essential in assessing progress and identifying areas of improvement. These assessments need not be formal, intimidating exams but constructive, positive experiences that guide and encourage students. Your curriculum should accommodate regular feedback sessions with students.

Areas to emphasize while giving feedback:

- Progress in technical skills and theory knowledge.

- Performance readiness.

- Creativity and improvisational skills.

A thoroughly planned, balanced, and adaptable curriculum forms the backbone of any successful music academy. Remember to embrace flexibility, promoting individual journeys in music learning while adhering to the foundational structure your curriculum provides. Above all, foster a love for music in your academy that goes beyond mastery and technique and nurtures a lifelong passion for this sublime art form.

Chapter 7. Harmonizing Logistical Hurdles: Solving Operational Challenges

The first notes of your entrepreneurial opera will most certainly involve confronting and harmonizing operational challenges. Although daunting, these initial hurdles are necessary preludes, setting the tenor for your future success.

7.1. Unraveling Key Challenges

Like every business venture, a music academy has its share of operational challenges. While these range from managing administrative work to maintaining a conducive learning environment, they all require sound solutions to ensure a symphony of success.

One of the key challenges includes managing the vast administration work that comes with running a music academy. This could involve coordinating lesson schedules, concerts, and examinations, keeping student records, handling finances, and much more. Not surprisingly, keeping up with all of these tasks can eat into the time that should be spent nurturing and mentoring students, a situation you'd certainly want to avoid.

Another hurdle is the need for a nurturing and conducive learning environment. The importance of physical space in learning music extends beyond just having a quiet, comfortable area for students to practice. Acoustic considerations, availability of different instruments, and access to technology for digital music production also come into play.

Also, putting together the right tutors who are not only accomplished musicians but also passionate educators is essential. A thriving music academy needs instructors who can inspire learners and can tailor their approaches to accommodate students' varied learning styles and pace.

Finally, marketing your music academy and balancing finances can be tricky. As with any other business, having a steady stream of students is critical to your academy's survival and growth. At the same time, maintaining financial stability is paramount while offering competitive rates to attract and retain students.

7.2. Administering the Symphony

Now that we've outlined the chief challenges, let's dive into solutions.

A thoughtful administrative system is integral to manage the numerous tasks associated with your music academy. To streamline administrative tasks, consider integrating specialized music school management software into your setup. Such software can handle lesson scheduling, billing, attendance tracking, communication with parents, and more, freeing up time to concentrate on the musical heart of your academy. Efficient use of technology can turn daunting administrative duties into harmonious tasks, improving overall productivity.

Also, delegating responsibilities among staff can distribute the workload evenly. Encourage staff members to take ownership of their responsibilities, turning them into managers of their 'sections' within the larger 'orchestra' of the music school.

7.3. A Conducive Concerto

When it comes to providing a conducive learning environment, the design and layout of your academy play a significant role. Classrooms should be soundproofed to ensure isolation during lessons and practice sessions. Additionally, invest in quality music instruments and technology to aid in teaching and learning.

Spaces for relaxation and socializing, like a lounge or garden, can foster camaraderie among students, making your academy not just a place for learning but a community of music lovers. Remember, the best music is often made when musicians are comfortable, relaxed, and inspired.

7.4. Assembling A Harmonious Ensemble

Finding the right tutors is not a mere task but an art form of recruitment. To attract proficient teachers, consider offering competitive salaries, a conducive work environment, opportunities for professional development, and the flexibility to express their teaching styles. Once on board, hold regular meetings to ensure their alignment with the academy's educational goals.

Also, don't forget the power of continuing education for your teaching staff. Workshops, seminars, webinars, and collaboration platforms can be part of professional development programs. This not only enhances your teachers' skills but also reinvigorates their passion, which is ultimately transferred to their students.

7.5. Crafting A Mélange of Music and Marketing Magic

Regarding marketing, clever strategies are your chorus here. Capitalize on digital marketing platforms to reach a broad audience. Create an appealing, user-friendly website for your academy, showcasing your facilities, faculty, curriculum, success stories, and more. Stay active on social media, consistently engaging with your audience and sharing relevant content. Running special campaigns, discounts, contests, or giveaways can also help attract potential students.

Direct marketing through community outreach, such as organizing free workshops or concerts, can be another useful tactic. Word-of-mouth from satisfied students can supplement these efforts.

On the financial front, create a robust budget plan covering all operational costs, salaries, utility bills, maintenance, and marketing expenses. Monitor your academy's in and outflows regularly and adjust your plan as necessary. Offering varied pricing models based on students' levels, group or individual lessons, and commitment can also help maintain a steady revenue stream.

7.6. Turning Dissonance into Harmony

Embarking on a journey to build your music academy will involve some dissonance. However, embracing operational challenges as part of your entrepreneurial symphony can transform them into subtle yet powerful harmonies that ultimately crescendo into your academy's fruitful melody. Remember, as an entrepreneur, you're not only the conductor but also the composer, writing your academy's unique score. Therefore, the way you solve logistic hurdles can become your signature tune, setting your venture apart from the rest.

Chapter 8. Amp Up Your Marketing: Attracting Aspiring Musicians

The journey begins here, in the throbbing heart of your music academy: marketing. Let's focus on attracting your first batch of aspiring musicians who will define the brand of your academy for the years to come.

8.1. Building Your Brand Identity

First and foremost, solidify your music school's brand identity. Identify what sets you apart from other music schools. Your unique appeal could be an exclusive course you offer, a world-renowned faculty member, or simply how you present your school's atmosphere. This identity creates the vibe and tone for all aspects of your academy, including your logo, color palette, online presence, and marketing materials.

8.2. Developing an Attractive Website

In the age of the internet, having an appealing, user-friendly, and engaging website is a must. Your website should provide information about you, your team, your mission, and the courses you offer. Make sure your website is updated regularly with captivating content like blog posts, music tutorials, or faculty interviews that can draw in visitors regularly.

8.3. Utilizing Social Media Platforms

Social media is a key player in marketing strategy. Make use of the platforms where your target audience spends most of their time, like Instagram, Facebook, YouTube, or LinkedIn. Deliver engaging content like behind-the-scenes videos, student performances, and testimonials. Moreover, contests and giveaways are excellent ways to increase engagement. Remember to interact with your followers by responding to comments and messages.

8.4. Working with Influencers

Working with influencers who align with your brand can have a significant impact. Local musicians, music teachers, or music influencers could share your content or tag your school, providing a greater reach and potentially attracting more students.

8.5. Leveraging Search Engine Optimization

Make sure your website and content are search engine optimized. Incorporating the right keywords and phrases related to music learning and education in your area can improve your visibility on search engines, attracting more local students.

8.6. Running Local Advertisements

If your budget allows, run local advertisements in newspapers, radio, and even local TV channels. Strategically placed ads can lead to substantial regional awareness, drawing in interested students.

8.7. Offering Free Trials

Offering a free trial class or workshop is a great way to hook prospective students. The trial should be an unforgettable experience, showcasing your school's quality of teaching and atmosphere.

8.8. Organizing Open Days or Music Events

Hosting an open day allows potential students and their parents to experience the academy's environment firsthand. Regularly organized music events can be another excellent way for prospective students to witness the progress and performances of current students.

8.9. Referral Program

Word of mouth is a powerful marketing tool. Encourage this by creating a referral program where current students or families receive discounts or rewards for every successful referral.

8.10. Collaborating with Schools

Liaise with local schools for performances or workshops. Schools often look for such collaborations for their cultural events, and your academy could offer voluntary or paid music services, creating a good rapport and visibility among potential students.

8.11. Engaging in Community Services

Participate in city events, charity shows, or local concerts voluntarily. This not only makes your institution recognizable but also builds a positive reputation within the community.

While executing these strategies, remember to leverage your unique selling proposition and consistently communicate your value across all platforms and mediums. Don't try to imitate other schools; instead, let your school's personality and strengths shine. Always be patient and persistent with marketing efforts. It might take some time, but with determination and persistence, you'll see a steady increase in enquiries and enrollments.

In the end, remember that your goal is to transform these aspiring musicians into accomplished artists. Your marketing efforts are merely a means to that rewarding end. On that high note, let's move towards building a worthwhile curriculum and an ambiance that strikes a chord with every aspiring musician who walks into your academy. Tune in for the next section.

Chapter 9. Studio to Symphony Hall: Charting Progress and Growth

At the commencement of your music school journey, mapping out a clear path for students, from their first note strummed in a humble studio to a grand performance in a symphony hall, is immensely crucial. It underpins not just the musical training that they partake but also their broader transformation into accomplished musicians.

9.1. Setting Up Your Music Studio

The music studio is the incubator where fledgling musicians will begin to shape their skills and find their creative voice. The initial step is to select a suitable location for your studio. It should be in a serene, quiet locality to ensure undisturbed practice sessions, and the acoustics must be top-notch. Acoustic panels, diffusers, and bass traps can help attain the desired sound quality.

Ensure the studio is resplendent with musical instruments of all kinds - from guitars to grand pianos, violins to flutes. The practicing musician should feel inspired in their musical cocoon, with relatable aesthetics, motivational quotes, and music-related artwork.

9.2. Crafting the Curriculum

The soul of your music academy will be its curriculum. The design must be such that it caters to the diverse needs of students - beginner, intermediate, and advanced. Stick to a harmonious blend of theory and practice, with enough scope for creativity.

While tailoring the curriculum, remember not to overwhelm your students with rigorous, marathon lessons. Instead, adopt a gradual and steady pace. The progress may seem slow initially, but maintaining a student-friendly tempo helps in thorough understanding and longer retention.

9.3. Ensuring Growth and Development

To ascertain whether the students are growing as musicians, frequent assessments, feedback sessions, and performance opportunities in-house are indispensable. Constructive feedback is necessary to make necessary modifications in the training to help them improve better.

Additionally, fostering a sense of community within the music academy can spur progress significantly. Enable regular jam sessions, collaborative projects, or music competitions where the students can display their learnings, and hone their craft, while enjoying the process.

9.4. Molding Performers: The Transition to Symphony Hall

The journey towards the Symphony Hall represents the pinnacle of the musical trajectory. The aim is to create a space where aspiring musicians gain the confidence to exhibit their musical prowess in front of a larger audience. Arranging for music recitals or community concerts can be the first step towards this dream.

Transforming a studio musician into a concert performer requires more than just technical knowledge. Students need to be equipped with stage presence, familiarity with different performance spaces, and the ability to handle stage fright.

9.5. Continuing Education & Lifelong Learning

Establishing a culture of continuing education and lifelong learning is the secret ingredient to grow as a musician. Encourage students to consistently expand their skills beyond your music school. Motivate them to participate in music workshops, symposiums, and master classes that offer different perspectives and enrich their musical panorama.

The journey from studio to symphony hall is both miraculous and strenuous. But with a robust structure, a light-filled pathway, and ceaseless dedication, creating this journey becomes an achievable dream. As they say in the realm of music, every professional was once an amateur, every symphony hall musician, a beginner in the studio. It's the wise guidance, practiced patience, and nurturing environment of the music school that makes this transformation possible.

And as you traverse this journey with budding musicians, remember to enjoy every note, every symphony, and all the music that fills your academy. Because that, after all, is your real achievement - to create a space that resonates with the harmonious echoes of aspiring musicians, guiding them towards their musical zenith.

Chapter 10. Encore Performance: Retaining Students and Staff

In any institution of learning, retention is a key indicator of success. This chapter will dive into both aspects of retention important to a music school operation — retaining students and retaining staff.

10.1. The Virtuoso Symphony: Retaining Students

Retaining students is equivalent to keeping the lifeblood of your music academy pulsing. Consider these strategies to engage and retain your students.

10.1.1. Appreciate Individuality

Each student is unique and brings an individual flavor to your music academy. Acknowledge the individuality of every student, adapt to varying learning styles, and create an environment where each individual is valued and encouraged to express themselves.

10.1.2. Foster an Engaging and Welcoming Environment

The ambiance of your academy plays into the learning experience. An inviting and creative atmosphere stimulates open-mindedness, initiative, and a passion for learning. Providentially, music is a powerful thing that can facilitate these conditions.

10.1.3. Increase Parent Involvement

Parents play an instrumental role in determining a student's involvement in your academy. Make sure to engage parents in recitals, performances or parent-teacher meetings. This will keep them abreast of their child's progress and make them feel valued - cementing the relationship further.

10.2. The Guiding Conductors: Retaining Staff

Equally critical to your academy's success is keeping and nurturing talented staff. Here are some ways to enhance teacher satisfaction and prevent staff turnover.

10.2.1. Provide Competitive Compensation

This does not mean that you have to array your teaching staff with massive paychecks. Instead, ensure the compensation you provide is fair and competitive compared to others in the industry.

10.2.2. Offer Regular Training and Development Opportunities

Just as much as students need to learn and improve, so do your staff. Offering regular training programs, workshops or seminars keeps them well-acquainted with the latest trends and techniques in music education.

10.2.3. Recognize and Reward

Everyone appreciates a good pat on the back. Recognizing the efforts and successes of your team, whether through verbal praise, awards, or small perks, goes a long way in showing them that they are valued.

10.3. The Ongoing Encore: Continuing Education

One surefire way to keep both students and staff engaged is to ensure constant learning and growth. By motivating learners to perpetually stretch their abilities and deepen their understanding, you can create a thriving community eager to explore the music world further.

Promote ongoing learning through advanced courses, student recitals, workshops, and performances. Each of these endeavors allows students and teachers to showcase their continuous growth and progress within the academy.

10.4. Singing the Same Tune: Aligning Goals

It is essential to remember that aligning the goals of your students, your staff, and your academy is a crucial step towards their retention. It's all about creating harmony.

By openly communicating your academy's goals to students and staff, inviting feedback, and making necessary adjustments, everyone can sing from the same sheet of music, ensuring that all stakeholders stay aligned.

At the crescendo of our exploration into retention, the score is clear: successful student and staff retention is a balanced composition of respect, engagement, continuous learning, and collaboration. With these elements in place, your academy is set to enjoy many an encore performance.

Treat every day at your academy as an opportunity to perform, an opportunity for students to learn, and for staff to grow, inspire, and feel valued.

Remember, the sweetest music to your students and staff will be the rhythm of your academy's persistence, progress, and passion. Let them feel the melody everyday – the melody of a thriving music academy ready to nurture the musicians of tomorrow.

Chapter 11. Crowning Composition: Case Studies of Successful Music Schools

A successful composition, when it comes to a music school, is essentially the harmonious coalescence of multiple elements. It's about innovative pedagogy, nurturing learning environments, a strong vision, and the ability to amplify the potential of budding musicians. By examining the successful stories of established music schools, it's possible to decode the ingredients of this 'crowning composition' and apply them to your own entrepreneurial journey.

11.1. The Juilliard School: Legacy and Excellence

Founded in 1905, The Juilliard School in New York City stands as a shining example of achieving excellence in the space of music education. What sets Juilliard apart is its unwavering commitment to nurturing the artistic development of its students at every stage. This is ensured through a robust curriculum that encourages both, individual practice and ensemble performance.

Moreover, the strategic location of Juilliard - in the heart of a culturally rich city - provides students access to a thriving music scene, enhancing their educational experience. This reminder of the importance of location is not to advocate that every music academy needs to be at the city center, but to emphasise that accessibility to musical resources can greatly enrich the learning proposition.

11.2. Berklee College of Music: Embracing Evolution

Berklee College of Music, established in 1945, is best known as an institution that readily adapts to evolution within the music industry. What started off as an institution dedicated to jazz, has evolved to encompass a variety of modern styles as well as music technology. Its philosophy hinges on the belief that learning music isn't just about replications of old paradigm, but about pushing boundaries and breaking traditions to create novel soundscapes.

Additionally, Berklee's curriculum is deeply integrated with newer technologies for music training. Digital software is leveraged for compositions and performances, teaching students how to maximize their potential within the ever-evolving world of music.

11.3. Royal Academy of Music: Creating a Community

London's Royal Academy of Music has cultivated a sense of community which has played a pivotal role in its success. This institution promotes the idea of students learning not only from their instructors but also from each other. Building a network of musicians allows for collaborative learning and shared understanding.

Furthermore, outside their education, students also perform at various events, providing a platform to apply their skills and receive instant feedback from the audience.

11.4. The Curtis Institute of Music: Balancing Quality and Quantity

The Curtis Institute of Music classifies itself not just by its success, but by the means through which it achieves this success. With an acceptance rate of fewer than 5%, Curtis focuses intensely on individual student development, admitting only as many students as there are vacancies in its orchestras and opera productions.

The institute tenaciously ensures high-quality individual attention to every student. By limiting student intake, Curtis maintains a 2:1 student-faculty ratio, offering training that is not only top-notch but also highly personalized.

11.5. Guildhall School of Music and Drama: Diversification

Guildhall School has a comprehensive approach going beyond the traditional ambit of a music school, incorporating drama and technical theatre, and establishing it as one of the most respected institutions in the world. Its ability to diversify and integrate parallel art forms presents a clear example of how amalgamation can lead to an institution's growth and credibility.

These schools, with their unique philosophies and pedagogies, have managed to distinguish themselves in the field of music education. Draw inspiration from them and tailor these lessons to the suitability of your academy. They urge you to maintain excellence and integrity in teaching and administration, adapt quickly to changing trends, build a vibrant community, focus on individual attention, and remain open to diversification and parallel arts. With these lessons, your music academy too can play a symphony of success.